T0026025

BIOGRAPHIES OF DIVERSE HER...

JOHN LEWIS

STEPHANIE GASTON

TABLE OF CONTENTS

A Crabtree Seedlings Book

CRABTREE
Publishing Company
www.crabtreebooks.com

School-to-Home Support for Caregivers and Teachers

This book helps children grow by letting them practice reading. Here are a few guiding questions to help the reader with building his or her comprehension skills. Possible answers appear here in red.

Before Reading:

• What do I think this book is about?
  • *I think this book is about a real person named John Lewis.*
  • *I think this book will describe the important actions and decisions that John Lewis made.*

• What do I want to learn about this topic?
  • *I want to learn about the childhood of John Lewis.*
  • *I want to learn what civil rights means.*

During Reading:

• I wonder why...
  • *I wonder why John Lewis was interested in protecting human rights.*
  • *I wonder why John Lewis organized peaceful protests.*

• What have I learned so far?
  • *I have learned that John Lewis served in Congress for more than 30 years.*
  • *I have learned that in 1965, John Lewis marched for voting rights.*

After Reading:

• What details did I learn about this topic?
  • *I have learned that in 2011, John Lewis received the Presidential Medal of Freedom.*
  • *I have learned that John Robert Lewis died on July 17, 2020.*

• Read the book again and look for the glossary words.
  • *I see the word **justice** on page 3 and the word **Congress** on page 7. The other glossary words are found on page 22.*

JOHN LEWIS

John Robert Lewis was a leader in the fight for social **justice**.

Lewis dedicated his life to protecting human rights.

He was also an **activist** in the civil rights movement.

THE MEMORY OF ABRAHAM LINCOLN
IS ENSHRINED FOREVER

John Lewis is pictured second from right.

Lewis was a lawmaker for the state of Georgia.

He served in **Congress** for more than 30 years.

Lewis was born in Alabama on February 21, 1940.

He grew up during a time of racial **segregation**.

Even washrooms and water fountains were segregated.

In 1960, Lewis helped to organize peaceful protests for civil rights.

Many were sit-ins at restaurant lunch counters.

Lewis also helped to organize historic civil rights moments.

The Freedom Rides in 1961 were aimed at desegregating buses.

The March on Washington in 1963 was for jobs and freedom.

Martin Luther King Jr. delivered his famous "I Have a Dream" speech at the march.

The march for voting rights was in 1965.

Lewis and other activists walked from Selma to Montgomery, Alabama.

Lewis first ran for local office in Atlanta.

In 1986, Lewis was elected to the House of Representatives.

In 2011, Lewis received the Presidential Medal of Freedom.

John Robert Lewis died on July 17, 2020.

Glossary

activist (ak-tuh-vist): A person who brings about political or social change

civil rights (siv-uhl rahyts): The rights of citizens to political and social freedom and equality

Congress (kong-gris): The branch of the U.S. government that represents the American people and makes the nation's laws

justice (juhs-tis): Behavior or treatment that is fair and lawful

segregation (seg-ri-gey-shuhn): Setting someone or something apart from other people or things

Index